Sound of the Underground

Travis Alabanza

Co-created with Debbie Hannan

T0001858

methuen | drama

LONDON • NEW YORK • OXFORD • NEW DELHI • SYDNEY

METHUEN DRAMA
Bloomsbury Publishing Plc
50 Bedford Square, London, WC1B 3DP, UK
1385 Broadway, New York, NY 10018, USA
29 Earlsfort Terrace, Dublin 2, Ireland

BLOOMSBURY, METHUEN DRAMA and the Methuen Drama logo are trademarks of
Bloomsbury Publishing Plc

First published in Great Britain 2023

Cover image: Faith Aylward
Cover direction: Mia Maxwell

A catalogue record for this book is available from the British Library.

A catalog record for this book is available from the Library of Congress.

ISBN: PB: 978-1-3504-0623-0
       ePDF: 978-1-3504-0624-7
       eBook: 978-1-3504-0625-4

Series: Modern Plays

Typeset by Serena Grasso

To find out more about our authors and books visit www.bloomsbury.com and sign up for our newsletters.

THE ROYAL COURT THEATRE PRESENTS

Sound of the Underground

Written by Travis Alabanza
co-created by Debbie Hannan

Sound of the Underground was first performed at the Royal Court
Jerwood Theatre Downstairs, Sloane Square, on Thursday 19 January 2023.

Sound of the Underground

Written by Travis Alabanza, co-created by Debbie Hannan

Cast (alphabetical order)

CHIYO

Lilly SnatchDragon

Ms Sharon Le Grand

Mwice Kavindele as Sadie Sinner the Songbird

Rhys Hollis as Rhys' Pieces

Sue Gives A Fuck

Tammy Reynolds as Midgitte Bardot

Wet Mess

Co-Creator & Director **Debbie Hannan**
Designers **Rosie Elnile & Max Johns**
Lighting Designer **Simisola Majekodunmi**
Sound Designer & Composer **Alexandra Faye Braithwaite**
Musical Supervisor, Composer & Arranger **Martin Lowe**
Movement Director **Bambi/Omar Jordan Phillips**
Assistant Director **Femi Tiwo**
Associate Designers **Jacob Lucy & Tomás Palmer**
Music Associates **Nicola T Chang*, Tom Mitchell* & Jonathan Mitra***
Additional tracks produced by **Nicholas Gilpin**
Stage Manager **Jessica Thanki**
Deputy Stage Manager **Emma Skaer**
Assistant Stage Manager **Madeleine Coward**
Show Crew **Oscar Sale & Sam Kacher**
Wigs Supervisor **Sophia Khan**
Dresser **Adam Rainer**
Sound Operator **Florence Hand**
Radiomic Technician **Alice Brooks**
Outreach Coordinator **Lysander Dove**
Personal Assistant **Pia Richards–Glöckner**
Marketing Lead **Ellie Robinson**
Set built by **Royal Court Stage Department**
Scenic Art by **Gemstage**
Fabric Palace drapery by **Soft Tissue Studio**
Lighting hires by **White Light Ltd**

From the Royal Court, on this production:
Stage Supervisor **TJ Chappell–Meade**
Lighting Supervisor **Max Cherry**
Production Manager **Simon Evans**
Lead Producer **Chris James**
Sound Supervisor **David McSeveney**
Lighting Programmer **Stephen Settle**
Company Manager **Mica Taylor**
Costume Supervisor **Lucy Walshaw**

Act III:

for CHIYO
Costume Designer & Creator **Fancy Boy**

for Lilly SnatchDragon
Costume Designer & Creator **Joey A Frenette aka Bourgeoisie**
Wig by **Styled by Vodka**

for Ms Sharon Le Grand
Costume Designer & Creator **Max Allen**
Track produced by **Jonathan Mitra***

for Rhys Hollis as Rhys' Pieces
Track produced by **Nicola T Chang***
Costume Designer & Creator **Jivomir Domoustchiev**

for Mwice Kavindele as Sadie Sinner the Songbird
Costume Designer & Creator **Bambi Blue @ Trashy Planets**
Wig by **Sophia Khan**

for Sue Gives A Fuck
Costume Creator **Julian Smith**
Hat by **Noel Stewart**
Costume Designer **Sue Gives A Fuck**
Wig by **Wig Chapel**

for Tammy Reynolds as Midgitte Bardot
Wig by **Darren Evans**
Track produced by **Tom Mitchell***
Costume Designer & Creator **Alexandre Simões**

for Wet Mess
Costume Designer & Creator **Lambdog1066**

*members of the Musical Director Mentorship Scheme

The song **Sound of the Underground** is used with permission, written by Brian Higgins, Miranda Cooper and Niara Scarlett. Published by Xenomania Songs Limited, Honky Tonk Songs Limited (administered by Warner Chappell Music Limited) and Hipgnosis Songs Fund Limited (administered by Peermusic (UK) Ltd).

The Royal Court Theatre and Stage Management wish to thank the following for their help with this production: Anna Barcock, Blackout, Nick Blount, Maddy Collins, Tom Glenister, Henry Hayward, Sunita Hinduja, Sophia Horrocks, Djordje Jovanovic, Sarah O'Connor, Promptside, Young Vic, Zachary Willis.

Sound of the Underground

Written by Travis Alabanza, co-created by Debbie Hannan

Travis Alabanza (Writer)

Travis is a writer, performer and theatre maker from Bristol. Their writing, performance and public discourse centres on trans and Black identities.

For stage, Travis wrote and performed in their debut show Burgerz which won the Total Theatre Award at the Edinburgh Fringe Festival, sold out at Southbank Centre and Traverse Theatre and toured internationally. It was also voted one of The Guardian Readers Top Shows of The Year. The text is published by Oberon Books. Their play Overflow, which premiered at and streamed from The Bush, was met with critical acclaim including numerous four-star reviews and was shortlisted for the George Devine Award. Travis currently has a new show for stage in development with the Southbank Centre and Hackney Showrooms. Their latest theatre commission, Sound of the Underground, will premiere as part of the Royal Court's new season in 2023. For screen, Travis is developing projects with Lookout Point and Left Bank.

Travis' debut book None of the Above: Reflections on Life Beyond the Binary was published in 2022 by Canongate. 'A breath of fresh air ... There's no memoir like it' Independent

Travis' work has also appeared on BBC Front Row, The Verb and in 2019 they hosted their first radio documentary 'Going to The Gay Bar' for BBC Radio Four.

Their work has also earned them a place on Forbes' 30 Under 30 list 2021, on the Evening Standard's list of 25 most influential Londoners under 25 and on the Dazed100 list.

Debbie Hannan

(Co-Creator & Director)

As director, for the Royal Court: Pah-La, Latir (& Compania Nacional de Mexico), Primetime, Who Cares, Spaghetti Ocean, Peckham: The Soap Opera.

As assistant director, for the Royal Court: The Mistress Contract, The Nether, Teh Internet is Serious Business, Birdland, How to Hold Your Breath, God Bless the Child.

As director, other theatre includes: The Strange Undoing of Prudencia Hart (Royal Exchange, Manchester); Overflow (Bush); The Panopticon (National Theatre of Scotland); Little Miss Burden (Bunker); Thee Ugly One (Tron); Things of Dry Hours (Young Vic); Cuckoo, The Session (Soho); Shielders

(Traverse); Unprecedented – The Unexpected Expert (Headlong/BBC Arts/Century Films); Isolation (National Theatre of Scotland/Summerhall); Girl Meets Boy (Yard/National Theatre of Scotland); Lot & His God, Notes from the Underground (Citizens Theatre); Pandora (Etch/Pleasance); The Angry Brigade, The Wonderful World of Dissocia, liberty, equality, fraternity (RCS); After the Rhinoceros: The Red Pill, What We Know, Killer Joe, Conspiracy (RWCMD).

As associate director, other theatre includes: Our Ladies of Perpetual Succour (West End/International tour); Constellations (West End/UK tour); Little on the Inside (Clean Break).

As assistant director, other theatre includes: The Maids, Sleeping Beauty (Citizens); A Pacifist's Guide to the War on Cancer (Complicite/National); Enquirer, A Doll's House (National Theatre of Scotland).

As writer, theatre includes: Shame: A Double Bill (Bang Bang Bang Group); Vinyl Idol [co-writer] (Òran Mór).

As director, awards include: Genesis Future Director Award.

As associate director, awards include: Olivier Award for Best Revival (Constellations).

CHIYO (Performer)

CHIYO is a multi-disciplined Artist who is nicknamed the UK's Prinx of Provocation. Model, Dancer, and Drag King – CHIYO was the first Trans Man to compete for Mr Gay UK. Alongside producing sold out shows that vow to 'redefine sexy', CHIYO is fresh off stages like Wembley Stadium, and the O2 arena, having just come off tour with Becky Hill.

Instagram, @prinxchiyo

Lilly SnatchDragon (Performer)

Lilly SnatchDragon is an international, award – winning political comedy drag queen, burlesque artist and compere. Her approach to how the West stereotypes S.E Asian women won her 'Best Newcomer" at the London Cabaret Awards in 2015. She has been in the Top 10 'UK's most influential Burlesque Performers' since 2015, including No. 1 in 2017, No. 3 in 2018, No.5 in 2019 and recently voted No. 37 in the world for 2022.

Her most recent engagement was at the London Coliseum for the English National Opera and Improbable Theatre production of 'Cosi Fan Tutte'.

She is also one of the founders of sell-out show 'LADS' and of renowned all- Asian cabaret collective 'The Bitten Peach'.

Instagram, @lillysnatch

Ms Sharon Le Grand (Performer)

A nice cunt in a hat.

Instagram, @mssharonlegrand

Mwice Kavindele as Sadie Sinner the Songbird (Performer)

Mwice Kavindele is the artist behind Sadie Sinner The Songbird, and she is a creative force! Founder and curator of The Cocoa Butter Club, Sadie performs a seamless repertoire bursting with the RnB, Blues, Jazz, Motown, Funk and Neo-soul that raised her. Sadie brings entire rooms to their feet- her vocals and vibe, compelling them to dance the night away!

Mwice's legacy is creating productions to decolonise performance spaces and showcase and celebrate performers of colour. She also facilitates workshops and university lectures about reclaiming and redistributing the narrative of racially, gender and sexuality othered bodies.

Instagram, @sadiesinner

Rhys Hollis as Rhys' Pieces (Performer)

I'm a gender-fucking cabaret creature! A one stop cabaret troupe, multitalented, multi-award winning messy, smelly, fabulous, running late and putting on a show! I wanna mess with the conventions of what 'Theatre' is- I wanna be a part of shaking it up and smashing the world of cabaret with this theatrical realm. I wanna be there amongst my fellow nightlife darlings making magic and working with the mind of my good sis, Travis. I wanna do something new.

Instagram, @rhysspieces_

Sue Gives A Fuck (Performer)

I'm a failed actor turned drag queen turned possibly not failed actor? Travis Alabanza is amazing so I'd be part of anything they'd written but honestly it's just nice not to have to do hen do's for a bit.

Instagram, @suegivesafuck

Tammy Reynolds as Midgitte Bardot (Performer)

Midgitte is a robust liability. They have a beautiful singing voice that often brings an audience to tears while contemplating all the vivid possibilities life can bring us. Bardot is hilarious, and can often be found leaving crowds collapsed on the floor while their guts explode from laughter. They have phenomenal timing, dragging the emotions of spectators from joy to despair on the turn of a second. Their work can be acerbically, invoking a revolutionary zeal in the most inhibited of people, bringing new horizons of power, disgust, and the brute force of confronting our shared humanity on a dying planet. They also do drag.

Instagram, @midgittebardot

Wet Mess (Performer)

Wet Mess is a wet mess, horny for your confusion. Let it all out and guess again at the insecure balding white man/pussy prince/ alien baby. Have a lollygag, think about your fantasy flesh suits, call me sweet prince, and remember Roger in a kaftan. Choose to make some silly campy decisions, with all the hairy thems and dykey men. All I really wanna do is strip for the stripper and drive her home with the dogs.

Instagram, @wet_mess

Alexandra Faye Braithwaite (Sound Designer & Composer)

For the Royal Court: **Purple Snowflakes and Titty Wanks (& Abbey, Dublin)**.

Other theatre includes: **Bloody Elle (& Traverse), Wuthering Heights, Light Falls (Royal Exchange, Manchester); The Narcissist (Chichester Festival); Anna Karenina, Operation Crucible, Chicken Soup (Sheffield Theatres); Good Luck, Studio (Mischief/Mercury); Kes (Bolton Octagon); The Climbers (Theatre By The Lake); Things of Dry Hours (Young Vic); The Wonderful World of Dissocia, Shining City (Theatre Royal, Stratford East); Endurance (HOME); A Christmas Carol (Theatr Clwyd); My Name Is Rachel Corrie (Al Madina Theatre, Beirut); Cougar, The Rolling Stone, Dealing with Clair (Orange Tree); Dublin Carol (Sherman); Hamlet, Talking Heads, Rudolph (Leeds Playhouse); The Audience, Juicy and Delicious (Nuffield); Room (& Theatre Royal, Stratford East), The Remains of Maisie Duggan (Abbey, Dublin); The Cavalcaders (Druid); Toast, (& The Other Palace/Lowry), How Not To Drown, Enough (Traverse); When I Am Queen (Almeida).**

Madeleine Coward
(Assistant Stage Manager)

Theatre includes: **Birthmarked, Romeo and Juliet (Bristol Old Vic), South Western, Winners (The Wardrobe Ensemble), Cinderella, Great Expectations (Corn Exchange, Newbury), Dinosaurs and All That Rubbish (Edinburgh Fringe), Icarus, Fefu and Her Friends, The Place at the Bridge (Tobacco Factory Theatres).**

Events includes: **Bloomsbury Festival, The Theatre on The Downs (Bristol), The Journey to Planet Savalon, The Birthday Party Edition (The House of Savalon), The Museum After Dark (Bristol Museum), Royal Welsh College of Music and Drama Graduation Ceremony (St Davids Hall, Cardiff).**

This is her first production for the Royal Court.

Rosie Elnile (Co-Designer)

For the Royal Court: **A Fight Against (Una Lucha Contra...), Goats, Primetime 2017.**

Other theatre includes: **Violet (Britten Pears Arts); The Cherry Orchard, An Unfinished Man (Yard); Peaceaphobia (Fuel/ Commonwealth); Prayer, The Ridiculous Darkness, Unknown Island, The Convert (Gate); Thirst Trap (Fuel/Rachel Young); Run Sister Run (Crucible, Sheffield); [Blank] (Donmar); Our Town (Regents Park Open Air); The American Clock (Old Vic); The Wolves (Theatre Royal, Stratford East); The Mysteries, Three Sisters (Royal Exchange, Manchester); Abandon (Lyric, Hammersmith); Returning to Haifa (Finborough); BIG GUNS (Yard).**

Rosie is a performance designer and artist based between the UK and Portugal. She was a recipient of the 2020 Jerwood Live Art Fund.

Max Johns (Co-Designer)

Theatre includes: **Birthmarked (Bristol Old Vic/ MAYK); The P Word, Overflow, Strange Fruit, Rust (Bush); The Climbers (Theatre by the Lake); The Strange Undoing Of Prudencia Hart (Royal Exchange, Manchester); Once Upon A Time In Nazi Occupied Tunisia (Almeida); King John (RSC); The Panopticon (National Theatre of Scotland); Heartbreakin' (WLB Esslingen, Germany); Buggy Baby (Yard); Yellowman (Young Vic); The Half God of Rainfall (Kiln/ Birmingham Rep/Fuel); Wendy And Peter Pan (Royal Lyceum, Edinburgh); Kes, Random (Leeds Playhouse); Utility, Twelfth Night (Orange Tree); Enron, Our Town (The Egg); Life Raft, Medusa, The Light Burns Blue, Under A Cardboard Sea (Bristol Old Vic); Hamlet, All's Well That Ends Well (Tobacco Factory).**

Classical Music performance includes: **Fidelio (London Philharmonic Orchestra/Royal Festival Hall).**

Awards include: **BBC Performing Arts Fellowship 2015.**

Martin Lowe
(Musical Supervisior, Composer & Arranger)

For the Royal Court: **The Twits, Hope.**

Other theatre includes: **ABBA Voyage; Harry Potter & The Cursed Child, Once (West End/ Broadway); Pinocchio, The Light Princess, Nation, Caroline or Change, War Horse, (National Theatre); Mack The Knife–A Salzburg Threepenny Opera, Jedermann (Salzburg Festival); Our Ladies of Perpetual Succour, The Wolves in the Wall, Appointment with the Wicker Man (National Theatre of Scotland/ International) Jerry Springer the Opera (National/West End/Sydney); The Full Monty, Once On This Island, Mamma Mia! (West End/ International).**

Films include: **Mamma Mia! The Movie.**

Awards include: **Tony, Grammy, Olivier, Drama Desk, Obie and Helpmann Award (Once).**

Jacob Lucy (Associate Designer)

For the Royal Court: **Purple Snowflakes and Titty Wanks (& Abbey, Dublin).**

Other theatre includes: **Dead Air (Stockroom); The End of History (St Giles-In-The-Fields); The Enchanted (Bunker); Brixton Rock (The Big House).**

As co-scenographer, theatre includes: **Neverland (Parco Corsini, Italy).**

Simisola Majekodunmi
(Lighting Designer)

As lighting designer, for the Royal Court: **Is God Is, Living Newspaper.**

As associate lighting designer, for the Royal Court: **Shoe Lady.**

As lighting designer, other theatre includes: **A Christmas Carole (Trafalgar Studios); Treason: The Musical in Concert (Theatre Royal Drury Lane); Starcrossed (Wilton's Music Hall); Electric Rosary (Royal Exchange, Manchester); A Christmas Carol (Shakespeare North Playhouse); Nine Night (Leeds Playhouse); J'OUVERT (& Theatre503), Jungle Rumble (West End); Human Nurture (Sheffield Theatres); The Wiz (Hope Mill); Transformations (New Public); Driving Miss Daisy, Baby Box (Theatre Royal, York); Invisible Harmony (Southbank).**

As lighting designer, dance includes: **The UK Drill Project (Barbican); Traplord (180 Studios); Born to Exist (Netherlands/UK Tour); AZARA – Just Another Day & Night (The Place); Puck's Shadow (Watford Palace).**

As associate lighting designer, other theatre includes: **The Shark Is Broken, 15 Heroines (West End);**

Herding Cats (Soho); Carousel (Regent's Park Open Air).

Tomás Palmer (Associate Designer)

As designer, theatre includes: **Sophocles' Oedipus/ silent practice (LAMDA); The Wellspring [co-designer] (Royal & Derngate); Half Full, Coram Boy Opera (Bute, RWCMD); Winning (Glasgow School of Art); Time is Running Out (The Gate, Cardiff).**

As designer, opera includes: **Coram Boy Opera (Bute, RWCMD).**

As associate designer, theatre includes: **The Cherry Orchard (Yard); Word-Play (Royal Court).**

Awards include: **The Linbury Prize for Stage Design 2021, Andrew Lloyd Webber Foundation grant award 2020.**

Bambi/Omar Jordan Phillips
(Movement Director)

As movement director, theatre includes: **Sundown Kiki (Young Vic).**

As choreographer, theatre includes: **Marie Laveaux (Stanley Arts).**

As dancer, orchestral concert includes: **A Christmas Gaiety (Royal Albert Hall).**

As dancer, music videos include: **Love Me More (Sam Smith), Frankenstein (Rina Sawayama).**

As choreographer & performer, film includes: **'By Earth Sea and Air, The heart wants what the heart wants (Adham Faramawy); Life Cycles Of Rainbows (India Sky).**

As producer: **The Black Obsidian Ball, at Rivoli Ballroom (part of We Are Lewisham, presented by Lewisham Council & the Albany as part of the Mayor's London Borough of Culture 2022).**

Omar Jordan Phillips is a creative producer, community organiser and movement artist, interested in driving artistic work for social change. Bambi quickly became a cornerstone of the London Ballroom Scene, where she is a part of the iconic, Unforgettable House of Revlon and Mother of the Kiki House of Laveaux. Bambi believes in Voguing as a form of social activism - a direct connection to trans embodied ancestry. She creates work that explores identity and the deconstruction of learned ideas of gender, sexuality, desire and race.

Emma Skaer
(Deputy Stage Manager)

For the Royal Court: **Let the Right One In, Total Immediate Collective Imminent Terrestrial Salvation (& National Theatre of Scotland).**

Other theatre includes: **Burn, Orphans, The Panopticon, My Left/Right Foot, The Reason I Jump, Adam, The 306: Day, Last Dream on Earth, The James Plays, The Driver's Seat, Macbeth, Enquirer, An Appointment with the Wicker Man, Knives in Hens, Girl X, The House of Bernarda Alba, Dolls, The Bacchae, Wolves in the Walls, (National Theatre of Scotland); Inadmissible Evidence (Donmar); All My Sons, Sunshine on Leith (Dundee Rep); How to Fix a Broken Wing, Ugly Duckling, The Book of Beasts, Something Wicked This Way Comes, Hansel and Gretel (Catherine Wheels Theatre Company); The Secret Garden, Black Beauty (Red Bridge Arts); If These Spasms Could Speak (Robert Softley Gale/The Arches); The Shape of Things (Starcatchers/Branar); Kind of Silence (Solar Bear).**

Opera includes: **Pop Up Opera (Scottish Opera).**

Jessica Thanki (Stage Manager)

For the Royal Court: **Living Newspaper Edition 4, Inside Bitch, Take Up Space, Broken Dreams.**

Other theatre includes: **Maybe Father (Talawa/ Young Vic); Behna (Kali/Birmingham Rep); It Hasn't Happened Yet (UK tour); Brixton Rocks (Tara Arts/UK tour); Dea (Sutton Theatre); The Ruck (Lawrence Batley Theatre/UK tour); Tales of Birbal (Mashi, UK tour); Clockwork Canaries (Theatre Royal Plymouth/The Drum); Cathy (Cardboard Citizens/UK tour); Muddy Choir (Theatre Centre, UK tour); We're Going on a Bear Hunt (UK/International tour); Gruffalo's Child (International tour); Josephine (The Egg, Bath); The Lion, The Witch and The Wardrobe (UK tour); 101 Dalmatians (Regents Park Open Air Theatre); Famous Five (Theatr Clwyd, Chichester Festival).**

Jessica has been shortlisted for Stage Manager of the year in 2011, 2018 and Stage Management Team of the Year 2019.

Femi Tiwo (Asssistant Director)

As writer, theatre includes: **Rights for whom, exactly? (Young Vic/Fly The Flag).**
As writer, director & actor, film includes: **Cab Ride.**

As actor, theatre includes: **Parakeet (Boundless/ Roundabout); Little Miss Burden (Bunker); And The Rest of Me Floats (Bush).**

As actor, film includes: **Losing Joy, Ackee and Saltfish, Faces, We Love Moses, The Ting.**

Femi Tiwo (FKA Michelle) is a multi-disciplinary artist. Their work spans radio, poetry, theatre, film, fashion and music. There is no art form off-limits when it comes to fully realising the perspective of this emo with a sunshine aura.

THE ROYAL COURT THEATRE

The Royal Court Theatre is the writers' theatre. It is a leading force in world theatre for cultivating and supporting writers – undiscovered, emerging and established.

Through the writers, the Royal Court is at the forefront of creating restless, alert, provocative theatre about now. We open our doors to the unheard voices and free thinkers that, through their writing, change our way of seeing.

Over 120,000 people visit the Royal Court in Sloane Square, London, each year and many thousands more see our work elsewhere through transfers to the West End and New York, UK and international tours, digital platforms, our residencies across London, and our site-specific work. Through all our work we strive to inspire audiences and influence future writers with radical thinking and provocative discussion.

The Royal Court's extensive development activity encompasses a diverse range of writers and artists and includes an ongoing programme of writers' attachments, readings, workshops and playwriting groups. Twenty years of the International Department's pioneering work around the world means the Royal Court has relationships with writers on every continent.

Since 1956 we have commissioned and produced hundreds of writers, from John Osborne to Jasmine Lee-Jones. Royal Court plays from every decade are now performed on stage and taught in classrooms and universities across the globe.

We're now working to the future and are committed to becoming carbon net zero and ensuring we are a just, equitable, transparent and ethical cultural space - from our anti-oppression work, to our relationship with freelancers, to credible climate pledges.

It is because of this commitment to the writer and our future that we believe there is no more important theatre in the world than the Royal Court.

Supported by
ARTS COUNCIL ENGLAND

🐦 royalcourt 📘 royalcourttheatre

ASSISTED PERFORMANCES

Captioned Performances

Captioned performances are accessible for people who are deaf, deafened & hard of hearing, as well as being suitable for people for whom English is not a first language.

Sound of the Underground: 8 February 7.30pm

Graceland: 3, 10 March 7.45pm

BLACK SUPERHERO: 12, 19 April 7.30pm, 27 April 2.30pm

BSL-interpreted Performances

BSL-interpreted performances, delivered by an interpreter, give a sign interpretation of the text spoken and/or sung by artists in the onstage production.

Sound of the Underground: 22 Feb 7.30pm

ASSISTED PERFORMANCES

Audio-described Performances

Audio-described performances are accessible for people who are blind or partially sighted. They are preceded by a touch tour which allows patrons access to elements of theatre design including set and costume.

Sound of the Underground: 25 Feb 2.30pm with TT at 1pm

BLACK SUPERHERO: 29 April 2.30pm with TT at 1pm

ASSISTED PERFORMANCES

Performances in a Relaxed Environment

Relaxed Environment performances are suitable for those who may benefit from a more relaxed environment.

During these performances:

– There is a relaxed attitude to noise in the auditorium; you are welcome to respond to the show in whatever way feels natural
– You can enter and exit the auditorium when needed
– We will help you find the best seats for your experience
– House lights may remain raised slightly
– Loud noises may be reduced

Sound of the Underground: 18 Feb 2.30pm

Graceland: 11 March 3pm

BLACK SUPERHERO: 22 April 2.30pm

If you would like to talk to us about your access requirements, please contact our Box Office at (0)20 7565 5000 or boxoffice@royalcourttheatre.com
The Royal Court Visual Story is available on our website. Story and Sensory synopses are available on the show pages via the Whats On tab of the website shortly after Press Night.

COMING UP AT THE ROYAL COURT

Thu 09 Feb–Sat 11 Mar
GRACELAND
By **Ava Wong Davies**
Graceland is a co-production with SISTER

Tue 14 Mar–Sat 29 Apr
BLACK SUPERHERO
By **Danny Lee Wynter**

ROYAL COURT SUPPORTERS

The Royal Court Theatre relies on the support we receive from individuals, trusts and corporate partners to help us to achieve our mission of supporting, nurturing and empowering writers at every stage of their careers. Through our writers, we are at the forefront of creating restless, alert, provocative theatre that reflects the world in which we live and our mission is more important than ever in today's world.

Our supporters are part of the essential fabric that enables us to keep our finger on the pulse – they give us the freedom to take bigger and bolder risks, challenge the status quo and create world-class theatre that affects and disrupts the theatre ecology. It is through this vital support that the Royal Court remains the writers' theatre and that we can continue to seek out, develop and nurture new voices both on and off our stages.

Thank you to all who support the Royal Court. We really can't do it without you.

BAR & KITCHEN

The Royal Court's Bar & Kitchen aims to create a welcoming and inspiring environment with a style and ethos that reflects the work we put on stage.

Offering expertly crafted cocktails alongside an extensive selection of craft gins and beers, wine and soft drinks, our vibrant basement bar provides a sanctuary in the middle of Sloane Square. By day a perfect spot for meetings or quiet reflection and by night atmospheric meeting spaces for cast, crew, audiences and the general public.

All profits go directly to supporting the work of the Royal Court theatre, cultivating and supporting writers – undiscovered, emerging and established.

For more information, visit
royalcourttheatre.com/bar

HIRES & EVENTS

The Royal Court is available to hire for celebrations, rehearsals, meetings, filming, ceremonies and much more. Our two theatre spaces can be hired for conferences and showcases, and the building is a unique venue for bespoke events and receptions.

For more information, visit
royalcourttheatre.com/events

Sloane Square London, SW1W 8AS ⊖ Sloane Square ⇌ Victoria Station
🐦 royalcourt f theroyalcourttheatre ⊙ royalcourttheatre

SUPPORT THE COURT AND BE A PART OF OUR FUTURE.

Every penny raised goes directly towards producing bold new writing for our stages, cultivating and supporting writers in the UK and around the world, and inspiring the next generation of theatre-makers.

You can make a one-off donation by text:

Text **Support 5** to 70560 to donate £5

Text **Support 10** to 70560 to donate £10

Text **Support 20** to 70560 to donate £20

Texts cost the donation amount plus one standard message. UK networks only.

To find out more about the different ways in which you can get involved, visit our website: royalcourttheatre.com/support-us

The English Stage Company at the Royal Court Theatre is a registered charity (No.231242)

Sound of the Underground

Author's Note
By Travis Alabanza

I would not be where I am today, meaning making art, without
London queer nightlife
I would not be where I am today, meaning not afraid of who I am,
without London queer nightlife
I would not be where I am today, meaning alive, without London
queer nightlife.

When I was beginning to call myself an artist, I was often put into
rooms that made me feel like I couldn't do it. Maybe the room was
too stuffy, or the faces too pale. Something would happen to cause
a lump in my throat. The lump could be called imposter syndrome
online, or it could be called 'I'm fucking faking it' by my inner
voice, or maybe it is just called 'not feeling like the posh kids' in
a room (read: industry) made up of Oxbridge grads and hand-me-
down privileges.

But there is one place I always felt like I *could* do it. That I *could*
make it. That I *could* put it on stage: the clubs.

I am not formally trained, in the sense that I do not have a degree,
nor did I go to a drama school; but I am trained in the sense that I
have been taught. I have been taught how to make a room fall to
silence with one look. Then to make them laugh with just a turn of
your mouth. How to carry on performing even if a hen do erupts in
a fight. How to make sure a hen do erupts in a fight. Through the
friendships made, the dressing room lessons, the stern words from
elders by the bar, the London queer nightlife taught me so much
about the art of theatre. Whether at The RVT, Her Upstairs, The
Glory, Dalston Superstore, VFD, I was given an understanding of
what community is. Messy. Entangled. Glorious. Connected. Fragile.
Evolving. And forever with you even after you try to leave it.

So, I join the many queer artists who salute the sticky basements
and stickier toilets for their education and follow a lineage of those
artists who are so entranced by that surrounding they must make
art about it.

Introducing: *Sound of the Underground.*

I thought this would be a play about nightlife and a homage to the people who keep it going. I guess it is in some ways. In the way that to put anything on a stage is a homage. But I would say this is less a play about nightlife in general, and more a play that turned into wondering how we make art again. How do we collaborate? How do we get paid? How do we keep up with all the changes within live work and performance? How do we continue to do it when it all feels so tough?

I wanted to ask these questions, by gathering the very people who made me feel like making art was possible. To see if we could figure it out together. I wanted the people who come from a world that has always continued, and burned brighter no matter the fire around it, to give us the answers. Or at least, some of them. If we didn't have the answer: at least I knew they'd still put on a fucking good show.

Introducing… *Sound of the Underground!*

Director's Note
By Debbie Hannan

They are not your family; they are your employers. Know your
rights. And, crucially, know how much everyone is getting paid.
– Salome Wagaine. 'Programme Note' on Peeled and Portion
Substack, March 2022

You better work. – RuPaul, Supermodel, 1993.

Yes Ru, but how?

The current crisis in Britain, in art, in the clubs, is one of work.

Who works, where we're allowed to work, those paid little for vital
work, those who receive bonuses off the backs of others' work,
those who tax our work and use that money for corrupt means,
and those whose work isn't considered any kind of work at all, but
more of a frivolous hobby.

When work stops enabling you to live, what then?

We wanted this show, and the process of making it, to be a
transformation.

Theatre often talks about progressive change, without enacting it.
Making *Sound of the Underground* was, instead, a direct action. This
meant interrogating every element of labour and articulating what
we wanted to change. We wanted it to be fairer. We wanted to work
more collectively. We wanted all types of humans to work safely on
our show. We wanted to respect club, drag and working-class forms,
and not squash ourselves into a middle-class dramaturgy. And we
wanted to make art that represents these values but also has them
sewn through the very muscles of the work.

And we wanted all of it to be really fucking fun.

In real terms, this meant change starting with the paperwork. Activism can also look like a fair budget and an altered contract – and I had to begin in a vulnerable place, with my own role as Director. Travis and I being credited as co-creators was to better reflect our labour. The lines of certain roles in theatre are so often blurred, and job titles are more to denote areas of expertise and pay bands, than indications of who actually is doing what. So we wanted to expose that from the off, and reflect it in our payment – we are splitting the royalties between us equally. A small change on paper meant a significant change in how we work.

We also created job shares across multiple roles in the company, largely as a response to the need to create better models of working for those with chronic conditions and disability. We paid performers for work that took place before rehearsals. We scheduled in an unusual way that better suited these particular workers. We looked at how we could make sure money made it back to the queer club scene and its makers, so roles from costume to movement to participation were filled with experts from the scene. We ran an artistic process that had agency and autonomy built in. Rosie and Max lead a design process that went beyond reacting to a script, and was more like devising the show visually. We worked collaboratively across all departments. We lost any preciousness about whose lane is what, whilst acknowledging expertise.

And we talked about how much we're getting paid – and, sometimes painfully, how we felt about that.

This ultimately meant moving our consciousness towards our identities as workers, and letting that be a transformative, empowering shift. Yes, artists, yes, drag performers, yes, technicians, *and* also workers with rights. We are not enthusiasts, not hobbyists, and not the very lucky members of a community who need to accept the terms and conditions as punishment for electing to do such a 'silly' job. We are workers, who formed a collective, and made our art together for our audience.

We keep on showing our working – including in this playtext. By which I mean we keep exposing the assumed and default ways we make art, so we can build better ones. I'm not saying it was perfect – in fact, we definitely fucked it several times – but we tried, and here are the bones of it for you to take from and improve.

The ask that we put upon the team, from the producer Chris through to our designers, from our entire cast to our Assistant Stage Manager Maddie, from every costume designer to me and Travis too, meant more labour for all of us. It is far easier to work within the machine that's handed to you – the real work is changing systems, and I want to thank everyone involved for this work. Nothing about this show was the default – everything was a creation, an innovation, an evolution – which isn't easy, but absolutely is and was and will be the seed for change.

The line where art meets work is a fraught and porous boundary, ripe for exploitation and exclusion. As an artist from a working-class background, I know what that costs, and I can see who the industry abandons. But by building a more robust, sustainable way of working, we hope that *Sound of the Underground* offers another way.

With thanks to those who have influence my thinking about theatre-making as work: the blog posts of Salome Wagaine; the article *Theatre Enthusiast or Theatre Worker* by Medicore Dave; the A Good Night Out Reading Group; the play *Wild Bore* by Ursula Martinez, Adrienne Truscott and Zoe Coombs Mar; The TEAM's 'Economic Nutritional Chart'; Stef O'Driscoll, Nessah Muthy, Cat Shoobridge, Chris Sonnex, Matilda Ibini, Sophia Khan, Max Johns, Rosie Elnile and Vinnie Heaven.

Notes on the Design
By Rosie Elnile and Max Johns

On the design process
We experimented with a new approach to collaboration and the reuse of materials on *Sound of the Underground*, laying out some basic principles from the start: to collaborate with queer makers from the club and cabaret performance scene, to create the set and costumes predominantly from the remains of other shows, and to run the design process in tandem with the writing process in a back-and-forth of ideas, images, and text.

Images and elaborations on the design have been included after each corresponding Act.

A note for those that may want to put on this play, or study it, or think about it like that:
We first open auditioned over six hundred people from the London club scene. They were incredible. I am so thankful for their time. It shaped so much of the energy of this.

We then did a R&D in a week with the cast. This was about hearing what mattered to them, how they felt about their jobs, what interested them.

This text is just what we decided to do, on paper. It has a loose script that I created. It then has signs of the kind of structure that was made to hold the artists' decisions.

This was and is an open collaboration.

It changes and will change.

This is like the template.

It should change depending on the night/the people/the space it is performed in.

The show script should be taken with a shot of vodka or something non-alcoholic with the same. These are performers who make stuff their own. So, we must let them. Follow the text – but change a word to sound like you, play with the audience, and with each other.

Text is not the most important factor here, just one factor of many; bring yourself and who you are as an artist and maker.

Below is the script for what is on stage, with the particular performers we have cast, but the show is about the moment we come to the theatre. Think about it from the first experience to the end.

How does the theatre look when you enter? What do you hear? How have we left our mark?

All workings are encouraged to be shown. No need to hide anything, baby!

Remember: this is drag! Find your reveals, revel in the campery, enjoy the mess of it all.

Stage directions are in italics.

The Prologue: The Takeover

This is action that happens before the official show begins. From whenever the 'half' is called. The energy in the takeover should feel punk, provocative, playful and bold. The performers are in control, setting their rules.

Depending on cast energy levels, not all need to be always engaging in the takeover – some can be getting ready on stage, finishing touches, lying around rolling cigarettes.

On the balcony, watching people come in.

Sitting behind box office painting nails.

Not performing for anyone, but this idea of 'come to me'.

Midgitte *is making a cocktail at the bar and saying 'Well go, this whole thing ain't gunna start itself.'*

Ms Sharon *has the overhead announcement that says:*

Ms Sharon   Alright, alright, settle down settle down, this is your last chance to get to your fucking seats, you can leave now if you want but after that we lock the doors. Then you can still leave but you'll just look more like a prick if you do. You can do whatever you want with your phones, I'm not your mum, but if it rings, I have the right to answer. Only take photos of the cool bits, be as noisy as you fucking want this ain't a funeral, make sure to tag us on Instagram, and no videos unless you're gunna also send us money right into our PayPals. Now sit the fuck down cus I think we are ready to start.

*The cast (except **Midgitte** who is still making a drink in the bar) hurry in front of the traditional red-like theatre curtain which is hiding the set behind them.*

They stand in front of it, as if ready to begin, waiting for everyone to come in and sit. They are in their drag make-up, and 'rehearsal' 'outside' clothes; punk-esque, them as themselves out in public.

Despite quite a chaotic introduction they are all quite poised now, addressing the room with some seriousness about what is about to take place.

Ms Sharon   Right, now we're all here, we can get on with it. Sorry about the whole 'rah rah mean queers get you in your fucking seats' thing, just sometimes it feels like the only way you know how to treat an audience is like pets – lay down little treats in order to get the bum in the seat. Sometimes the treat is Phoebe What's-her-bridge reviving *Flea Balls* and other times it's the promise of queers acting all raucous and out of place. Tomato-tomahto. Anyway!

*The whole cast (bar **Midgitte** who is still outside) pull out a piece of paper or script from their pocket.*

They all give the welcome speech in that kind of 'speaking in front of assembly' tone.

Ms Sharon   Good evening, Royal Courtiers, my name is Ms Sharon Le Grand…

Well come on, it's not a fucking funeral… My name is Ms Sharon Le Grand… (*Clears throat and holds for applause.*)

To be or not to be, to be fucked or do the fucking, who gives a critic's asshole it is just lovely for us cross-dressing, queer delinquents to be above the ground for once. And to be here in front of you, at this fine, *royal* establishment. Like roots, planted in our filthy and sinful soil, we have grown, here… To you, the divine audience.

Chiyo   What's good, I'm Chiyo and I'm a drag king. I run a club night called Woof and I'm the sexual preference of every single one of you. As roots we hold potential, an ability to grow from dirt. Sometimes our roots are allowed to grow above the ground, if invited in, but normally only if we are programmed for a post-show performance on the other show's set – a show that is a loosely-themed queer play, featuring two white cisgender men who are allowed to peck on the lips and are basically straight if you blink hard enough, mmmmh liberation.

Sadie   Hi I'm Sadie, the songbird, I started the legendary Cocoa Butter Club! Sometimes, when roots grow into trees, or flowers, or fruits or vegetables – they are harvested, without the roots ever really getting credit. No one thinks about the root that grew the carrot, or that turned into flowers, or the Black drag queen who inspired Dua Lipa's makeup.

Rhys   My name is Rhys's Pieces, I run a cabaret night in London called Queerdos, it used to be called Queefy, if you're not sure what a queef is – ask your nan. If roots all start colliding under the soil, tangling with each other, competing for a crumble of sunlight, they can get in knots. We are putting our nightlife jobs on hold to be at this theatre, every night, we wanted to come up above the ground, leave the basements, the clubs, the parties, the cocai– (**Lilly** *slaps* **Rhys***'arm*) the companions, because things underground can get crowded, saturated, in need a bit of a shake-up.

Lilly   My name is Lilly SnatchDragon, I've been doing drag for over ten years, I'm also one of the founders of Bitten Peach. Even though the space above ground is expanding, it can feel like there is only enough oxygen for one type of plant. As the temperatures rise, and the conditions change, the roots turn on each other in order to survive. That can look like competing for water – or throwing each other in front of a bus in order to impress a straight person.

Sue   My name is Sue Gives A Fuck, and I really do, I give a fuck about our roots being allowed to grow, to blossom, and to share with you all about our club culture, history and the challenges that face our current community. I also care very

deeply about having four weeks off from entertaining drunk
women at hen dos.

Wet Mess   Before we begin, we would like to take this moment
to thank the Royal Court and all their donors for their sponsorship
that allows us to put on these plays. We will not question, single
out, or think too hard about where that money may come from –
and if we see any blood on our ten-pound note, we will simply
pretend it is nail varnish. Thank you.

There's a pause.

Rhys   Thank you Wet Mess,

Lilly (*whispering*)   Where's Midgitte?

Midgitte *bursts through the double doors. Big flashlight, big
energy, big vibes.*

Midgitte   Right, anyone got a lighter?

Pause...

Midgitte   Honestly, I won't be able to start this whole thing
without a cig. Pissed at myself cus I never forget a lighter,
always have at least two on me, one green and one red, see one
is for giving out and well the other one is for me. Well turns out
yesterday I got my colours mixed up and thought I still had the one
for me, so ended up giving one out to this guy at this party, nice
guy but not remarkable enough to describe, anyway, turns out I
actually must have already given out my other one – to this fit girl,
one of those indie girls still stuck in 2009 with a little helmet fringe
but she looks hot cus it's like, aww you're still doing all that whole
indie thing you would have been fun like ten years ago – I must've
given it to her cus when I went into my pocket when they called
the half, sorry – why the fuck did I just call it a half – anyway,
when they called half, I went to go find my lighter, it was all gone.
Can you fucking believe. And I been looking ever since. But yeah,

then I remembered, you're all here, and one of you must have a lighter. So why not just ask…not like we are in a rush. Nothing is ever urgent here.

Pause.

Midgitte   Go on, someone put one up in the air…

Midgitte *then waits for someone to volunteer. If there's multiple let's try* **Midgitte** *playing around with who they want to take the lighter from. Chance for audience play here.*

Midgitte *then climbs up on the stage – they enjoy the cig.*

Rhys *gives* **Midgitte** *the script that is their bit.*

Midgitte   Right, anyway, I'm Midgitte, Midgitte Bardot – and I'm also from the *spppooky* underworld, we are the roots, or whatever the fucking metaphor was. And yeah, we have a lot of stuff we wanna say, ooohhh we have a lot of stuff we wanna say, about the state of art, our art, our world, so we've come above ground – and we are doing it in the most radical way. Hauntingly timely, some would say. Scarily urgent, others may say. We have picked such a pertinent form to show you our feelings, that later, when you go home at night, and you are lying in bed next to your sex doll, and you close your eyes, and you usually think about the crossword, or if on Friday you can wear your fun, patterned socks – instead you will be thinking about us, and what we presented to you. And how urgent, timely and radical it was. So radical that in years to come you will be kept awake by the sheer power of everything we have to say.

What have we done, you say?

Well we've made a play!
So here it is…
OUR PLAY!

They all do a little bow. One holds up a sign that says 'APPLAUSE'.

As the cast go off stage, one of the cast members is heard saying, 'You didn't half fucking go on Midgitte.'

THE ULTIMATE HOCKEY JOKE BOOK

LAUGH YOUR "FACE OFF!"

Ian Robinson

MacIntyre Purcell Publishing Inc.

232 Fairmont Road, Cloverville, Nova Scotia B2G 2K9
www.macintyrepurcell.com | info@macintyrepurcell.com

Printed and bound in Canada by Rapido Books

Cover design: Denis Cunningham
Book design: Gwen North

ISBN: 978-1-77276-180-1

Library and Archives Canada Cataloguing in Publication

Title: The ultimate hockey joke book : laugh your "face off!" / Ian Robinson.
Names: Robinson, Ian (Broadcaster), author.
Identifiers: Canadiana 20230464165 | ISBN 9781772761801 (softcover)
Subjects: LCSH: Hockey—Juvenile humor. | CSH: Canadian wit and humor (English)—Juvenile literature. | LCSH: Wit and humor, Juvenile. | LCGFT: Humor.
Classification: LCC PN6231.H54 R63 2023 | DDC jC818/.602—dc23

MacIntyre Purcell Publishing Inc. would like to acknowledge the financial support of the Government of Canada and the Nova Scotia Department of Tourism, Culture and Heritage.

For my mother Barbara who introduced me to hockey by watching *Hockey Night in Canada* on Saturday nights, and for my father Tom for his unique sense of humour! And to my wife Roxanne for being the best hockey mom and to our retired hockey players Drake and Trent. Keep your stick on the ice!

1st PERIOD

Why did the chicken get kicked out of the hockey game?

Because of its fowl play.

What hockey legend loved doing
donuts on the ice?

Tim Horton.

What did the hockey player have
to eat at the BBQ?

Ice Burgers!

What did the Champions have for
dessert after the game?

Stanley CUP-cakes.

Why did they stop the zombie hockey game?

Because someone had a face off in the corner.

How do you scare hockey players?

You "DEKE" up on them.

Where do you always find
Connor Bedard?

At the "centre" of attention.

———————

Why did the hockey player go
to prison?

Because he shot the puck.

Why did the hockey player
get scared during their
first game?

They got cold feet.

What player always has Band-Aids in his wallet?

Darnell Nurse.

What do you call it when Santa plays the game?

HO HO HO-ckey!

What do you call it when a
hockey player skips school?

Playing "HOOOKEY."

What's white and blue and red
all over?

A Montreal Canadiens player!

Why was Cinderella such a bad hockey player?

Because her coach was a pumpkin.

Why did the hockey player go to the movie theatre?

To screen the goalie.

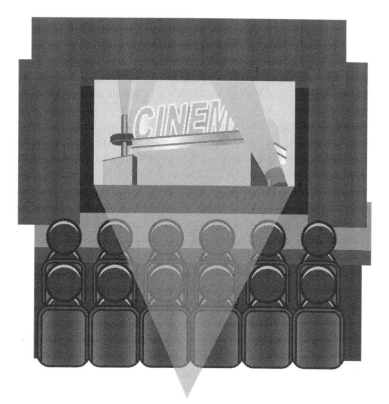

What player always has a cold?

Cole Caufield.

Why are hockey players good at
making friends?

*Because they know how to break
the ice!*

What penalty did the dog get?

Two minutes for RUFFING!

What's it called when a
T-Rex gets a goal?

A Dino-Score.

Why should you not tell jokes
while playing a hockey game?

Because the ice might crack up!

What did the hockey player
name their twins?

"Jock and Jill."

What part of the game
does the electrician like
most?

The "power" play.

Why does Brayden Point get
lots of goals?

Because he's always "on point."

Who did the moon
cheer for?

The shooting star.

What does a ghost wear at
Halloween?

A score sheet!

What team do you
NOT want to see while
swimming?

The San Jose Sharks!

Why don't hockey players
sweat much?

*Because they have too
many FANS!*

What penalty did the
fisherman get?

Two minutes for HOOKING.

How long do you have to
tickle the Detroit Red Wings
octopus before it laughs?

EIGHT tickles.

Where can you find a hockey
player in the park?

On the BENCH.

Who is the nicest player in the NHL?

Matthew Knies.

What NHL team is always treated
like royalty?

The Los Angeles Kings.

———————

What's the linesman's
best advice?

Keep it between the lines.

Who's the best player to
sail the hockey ship?

The CAPTAIN!

Where do zombies like to
hang out?

In the "ATTACKING Zone."

What do a doctor and a comedian
have in common with hockey
players?

They can both keep them in stitches.

Why should you date a goalie?

Because they're a KEEPER!

2nd
PERIOD

What does the
optometrist play?

"Eyes" hockey.

What do players for the New York Rangers have for a snack between periods?

A Big Apple.

What did the janitor put on their head to play hockey?

A "bucket."

How do hockey players stay clean?

With a "face wash."

―――――――――

What do hockey players call
their moustache?

Lip lettuce.

Why do Toronto players always think they are going to win the Stanley Cup?

Because they Be-LEAF!

What happens to a goalie when
they lose their keys?

They get SHUTOUT.

What player is always in trouble
with the officials?

Jesper Bratt.

———————————

What did one stick say to the
other stick?

"HIGH" stick!

Why did the hockey player
get arrested?

*Because they had two guns
and a six pack.*

What did the goalie glove say
to the blocker?

I've got you covered!

How do hockey players like
their drinks?

On ice.

What's David Pastrnak's
favourite pregame meal?

Pasta.

What NHL team did the pilot cheer for?

The Philadelphia Flyers.

What does the goalie use to paint a room?

MASKING Tape.

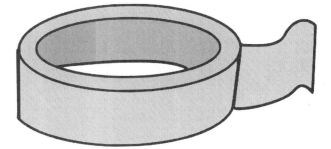

What's the referee's favourite
animal at the zoo?

The zebra.

What does Brad Marchand
like to toast at the campfire?

MARSH-mallows!

What does a Vegas player use to
cut his pregame steak?

A Golden Knife!

———————

Have you met my hockey friend?

Owen? O 'n five losses . . .

Where do hockey players
like to sit on a plane?

On the wings.

What's a hockey
player's favourite joke?

A "ONE-TIMER!"

Where do hockey players get their new uniforms?

New Jersey.

Why did the referee blow the whistle at Evgeny the player?

Because he knocked the Kuznetsov.

What can you catch from a hockey player?

Chicken pucks!

Did you hear about the
ghostbuster hockey player?

*They were good at blocking
GHOULS.*

The hockey team was glad they recruited a
ghost because it scored lots of ghouls.

What player absolutely loves
his family?

Nick Cousins.

Why can't pigs play hockey?

Because they HOG the puck.

What did the goalie say to the puck
after the warm up?

"Catch you later."

What do a dentist and a hockey
coach have in common?

They both use DRILLS!

Why couldn't the all-star
hockey players listen to music?

*Because they broke all
their records.*

Why don't hockey players go out on Halloween?

Because they'll be forced to take their FACE OFF!

What player goes to the rink on a motorcycle?

Nick Suzuki.

Ya know, hockey players are like goldfish.

The only real way to get their attention is to tap on the glass!

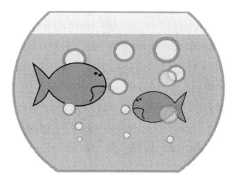

What position did the hockey ghost play?

A Ghouli!

What does the skeleton like
to do at the hockey game?

Watch the Zam-BONE-Y.

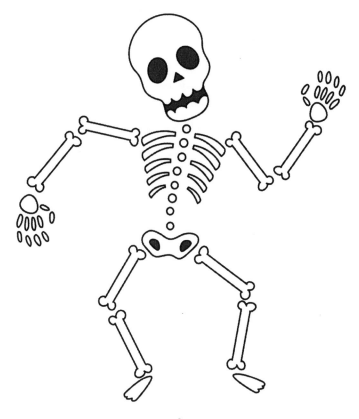

Why did the coach keep sending their players to the eye doctor?

Because they kept making blind passes.

What did the identical twins get for a penalty?

A "match" penalty.

Who did the goalie marry?

Annette.

Why did the team get
sentenced to prison?

They kept killing penalties.

What's Connor McDavid's
favourite hockey move?

The "McDeek-id."

What did the Coach say to the
slow-skating hockey player?

Get KRAKEN!

How did the goalie get a
sunburn on his neck?

Too much red light.

Why did the hockey player not want to go out?

Because they were a "Stay-at-HOME" defenceman.

What do you call it when a puck breaks the goalie's water bottle?

A little bottle rocket.

What do goalies hate to get
during a hockey game?

A SNOW shower.

How much wood could a
Tkachuck chuck, if a Tkachuck
could chuck wood?

Where did the Hockey Mom hide all the cookies?

On the "Top Shelf!"

What was the spine surgeon's favourite move?

"BACK-checking."

Where did the
electrician watch the
game?

*From the "CHERRY
picker."*

How did the soldier score all their goals?

With a "SNIPER" Shot.

What did the bug like to do during the hockey game?

Change on the "FLY!"

3rd
PERIOD

How do mice score all their goals?

Top cheese.

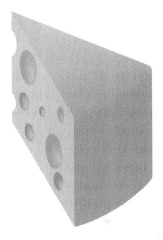

What did the bird do while
watching the hockey game?

"CHIRP" the players.

What is the favourite NHL team
of a mechanic?

The Oilers!

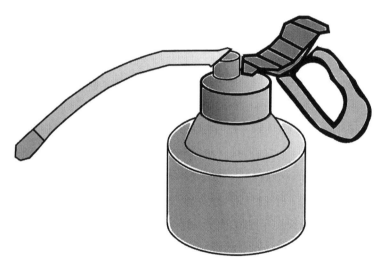

What are words of wisdom from the hockey player with the nice hair?

Just go with the "FLOW!"

What does the sanitation person like to score?

Garbage goals.

What team do ghosts
cheer for?

The Boston BOO-ins.

What did the hockey player
like to do at the beach?

Watch the "waves."

Why did the hockey player have
Alphaghetti after the game?

So they could catch some ZZZs.

What did Alex Ovechkin call
his album?

"8's Greatest Hits."

What does a goalie
have for breakfast?

Goose eggs.

What kind of goals
does a mechanic score?

Greasy ones.

What did the "show off
player" have for lunch?

A "hot dog."

Who do you want around when the power goes out?

A lamplighter.

———————

Why did the hockey player climb up the tree with a stick?

Because they wanted to play with the Maple Leafs!

———————

How do you keep a hockey player in suspense?

I'll tell you tomorrow . . .

Why couldn't the hockey
Captain learn the alphabet?

Because he got confused at C.

———————————

How did Han Solo score
his goals?

With a laser beam shot.

I'm worried about the hockey schedule.

Its days are numbered.

What does Connor McDavid always get for Christmas?

Nice mitts.

Why did the Detroit Red Wings octopus beat the San Jose Shark?

Because it was well-armed.

What happens when you put an Anaheim Duck in a cement mixer?

You get quacks in the pavement.

What do you call a rookie player
in San Jose?

A Baby Shark.

How do the Toronto Maple Leafs
like to play hockey?

Out on a limb.

Where does the nurse always sit
in the arena?

In the nosebleeds.

———————————

Knock knock.

Who's there?

Uriah.

Uriah who?

Keep Uriah on the puck!

Why did the hockey player take Buckley's cough syrup?

Because he was always coughing up the puck.

What does Sidney Crosby
use to sign his autographs?

A PEN-guin.

Seven days without playing
hockey can make one weak.

How did the criminal score
on their opponent?

By "picking his pocket."

What is the goalie's
favourite insect?

The butterfly.

What kind of supper does
the hockey player like?

"Puck" luck.

Why are swimmers good
at hockey?

Because they "dive" a lot.

What do you get when you cross a
goalie with the Invisible Man?

*Goaltending like no one's ever
seen before!*

What do you feed a rink rat?

Cheezies.

What's Leon Draisaitl's
favourite play?

Tic-Tac-GOAL!

How does the hockey player wake up for morning practice?

With a "stretch" pass.

Why do hockey players always carry an extra pair of skate laces?

Just in case they want to TIE the score.

How does the cook pass
the puck?

They "dish" it.

What do they clear the ice
with in Mexico?

With a "sand-boni."

How can you tell if hockey
officials are happy?

*Because they whistle while
they work.*

What is Frosty the Snowman's
favourite play in hockey?

"Snowing" the goalie.

Why didn't the skeleton
play hockey?

Because its heart wasn't in it.

How did the hockey goaltender
catch a fish?

With a NET!

Why didn't the dog want to
be a hockey player?

Because it was a boxer.

When should hockey
players wear armour?

*When they play
"KNIGHT" games.*

What do you call a hockey player who doesn't want to spend money?

A cheap skate.

What do you give a hockey player when they want more money?

A "CHECK!"

Why was the tiny ghost asked to join the hockey team?

Because they needed a little team spirit.

I kept wondering why the puck was getting bigger.

Then it hit me.

What do you call a hockey player with points in every game of the season?

A streaker!

OVERTIME

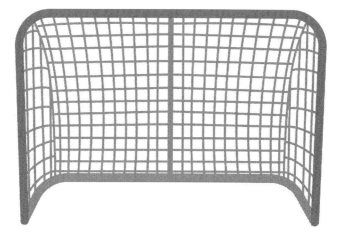

How do you stop squirrels from
playing hockey in the yard?

Hide the puck. It drives them nuts!

Why did the hockey player hold their skate boot to their ear?

Because they liked "sole" music!

———————

Why did the hockey player go to the washroom?

To go for a "PP."

———————

Why did the hockey player cross the rink?

To get to the other "slide."

Why shouldn't you play hockey in a jungle?

Because there are too many cheetahs!

What do you call a monkey who wins the Stanley Cup?

A CHIMP-ion.

Where did Jack Eichel
go on vacation?

To see the "Eichel" Tower.

What did the hockey player use to wash their car?

Their "bucket."

What do pilots do in their
spare time?

Play "air" hockey.

What do ducks use to tape
their hockey sticks?

Duct Tape.

What do hockey players do to celebrate a goal?

They dance the Hockey-Puckey.

What do hockey players eat when they fly?

Plain food.

Where did the gambler score all their goals?

From the "slot."

What do hockey players do
when they get overheated?

They move closer to the fans.

Why are goalies always doing laundry?

Because they love "clean sheets."

How can you spot a hockey linesman
at a birthday party?

*They are the ones who call the icing on
the cake.*

Did you hear about the terrible goalie that ran out in front of the subway train?

It went right through their legs.

Why did the baking club
show up at the hockey game?

*Because they heard there was
lots of icing.*

What does the goalie have with soup?

A biscuit.

What did the hockey
player see when they
got knocked out?

Three Stars.

What is the ghost's favourite
part of the hockey net?

The ghoul posts.

Ya know, you don't have to be CRAZY to be a GOALIE, but it sure helps!

What did the referee say to the hockey player they gave a warning to?

"I-cy" what you did there.

What did the little kid say to their mother during the intermission?

Where's POP-corn?

What position did the
plumber play?

Between the pipes.

———————————

What did the tape say to
the blade?

"We better stick together."

How does a hockey player kiss?

They PUCK-er up!

How did the janitor's team get eliminated from the playoffs?

They got "swept."

What penalty did the
carpenter get?

*Two minutes for
boarding.*

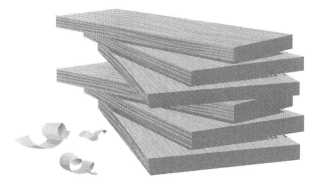

What do you call a Boston
Bruin player with no teeth?

A gummy bear.

What team does a firefighter cheer for?

The Calgary FLAMES!

What do you say to
the rabbit?

Nice Hockey "HARE!"

Why did the hockey player
bring string to the game?

So they could tie the score.

Why did the goaltender go
to the laundromat?

To get the crease out.

You know what team
really quacks me up . . .

The Anaheim Ducks.

What did the linesman do when they dropped their kids off at school?

They "waved" them off.

Why did the referee give the maple tree a penalty?

Because it was high sticking.

What's the favourite NHL team of the Weather Network?

The Tampa Bay LIGHTNING.

What NHL team is the hardest to tame?

The Minnesota Wild.

What did the hockey player
order when he went to the bar?

A *Slap SHOT!*

———————————

Why are carpenters afraid of
playing hockey?

*Because they're scared of getting
nailed to the boards.*

What piece of hockey gear
does the hunter love to use?

The "trapper."

———————

Which of Santa's reindeer does
a hockey player like best?

Dasher!

When do hockey players
wear dress suits?

When it's a TIE game.

What play does the alien make?

The SAUCER pass.

What does a hockey player say
at Halloween?

"Hat trick" or treat!

THE
SHOOTOUT

Hockey players and figure skaters don't date each other because nobody wants to break the ice.

———————————

What did the monkey say when his team won in quadruple overtime?

"That's bananas!"

When I was a hockey player going on road trips, I loved trying to pack myself into a small suitcase.

I could barely contain myself!

Where did the coal diggers
play hockey?

In the "Miner" Leagues.

What do you get from a hockey player after an argument?

A cold shoulder.

People can say that hockey zebras are carnivores but they would be lion...

Why is music like hockey?

If you don't "C sharp" you'll "B flat" ... on the ice."

What penalty did the
Knight get?

Five minutes for spearing.

What's the favourite chocolate
bar of a Boston Bruins fan?

A Bobby SKOR.

How would you describe the
butcher's style of hockey play?

A "Grinder."

What happened to the hockey player who got locked out of the locker room?

They felt ICE-O-Lated.

Why do hockey rinks always have curved corners?

Well, if they were 90 degrees the ice would melt!

Why was the tree at the rink?

So the players could ride the pine.

What's a hockey player's favourite pasta?

Zam-roni.

Where did the cows like to
play hockey?

In the "Old Barn."

What kind of hockey game does a
farmer prefer?

A Barn Burner!

What's the miner's favourite
part of the hockey stick?

The shaft.

————————

How did the hockey player's
scar heal?

"Overtime."

Why are scrambled eggs like a
losing hockey team?

Because they get beaten all the time.

What kind of vitamins
do goalies take?

Iron.

What did the bee say
when it got a goal?

"Hive" scored!

What players are always
looking for votes?

The Ottawa Senators!

What advice did the hockey dad give his son?

Don't go through life without goals.

Where do hockey coaches do their paper work?

In the off-ice.

Where did the hockey player like to drive their car?

In the "neutral" zone.

Before they invented the hockey drawing board, what did they go back to?

————————

The hockey referee rushed to catch his flight.

He got there when it was "two minutes for boarding."

Why are hockey players
so focused?

*Because they are "goal"
oriented.*

––––––––––––

What did the hockey official
study in class?

The face off circle.

What team did the cab
driver play for?

The Taxi Squad.

What did the hockey player say
after being checked hard?

That was a pain in the glass.

What did the pumpkin use to
protect its teeth?

A mouth "gourd."

Where did the goalie
put his bakery
purchases?

In the bread basket.

Which insect is best at hockey?

A SCORE-pion.

What NHL team does Dr.
Seuss cheer for?

The Detroit Red "THINGS!"

What do you call a bird that wins the Stanley Cup?

A CHIRP-ion.

Where do the hockey players buy their gear?

At the Yard CELLY.

The hockey team added a new player: the name is Seymour

. . . Seymour Goals.

Ya know something . . . the St. Louis Blues always hit the right notes!

What's a hockey player's least favourite beverage?

Penal-TEA.

The Zamboni drivers
disappeared at the local rink.

We hope they resurface soon!

———————————

What do hockey players like to
drink on a hot day?

An Ice Cap!

How did the hockey player deal with being traded?

They decided to stick it out.

What happened to the hockey players when they are cooking their pregame pasta?

They ran out of "thyme."

Which hockey player wears the biggest skates?

The one with the biggest feet.

What did Santa leave in Sidney Crosby's stocking when he was bad?

"Cole" Harbour.

What's the motto of hockey teams
from Finland?

You FIN some and you lose some.

———————————

What did the Columbus
groomsmen wear to the wedding?

"Blue Jackets!"

If three goals are a hat-trick, what do you call four goals by one player?

A "helmet" trick!

Ya know, hockey is a cool sport.

How do you know you got a gift
from a hockey referee?

*Because it came in a
"Penalty Box!"*

What did the cowboy ride to
the hockey rink?

A Zam-PONY!

Who is the Public Address
announcer's best friend?

"Mic."

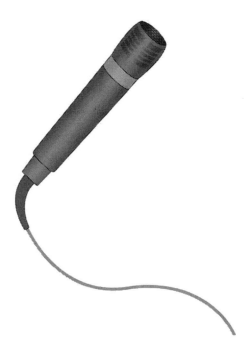

What was the barber's
favourite part of the
game?

The final BUZZER!